Dacyr Dante de Oliveira Gatto
Renato José Sassi

ITIL and BPM Integrated in the Software Release Process

ITIL and BPM Integrated in the Software Release Process

Dacyr Dante de Oliveira Gatto
Renato José Sassi

ITIL and BPM Integrated in the Software Release Process

Study in a Software Development Company

ScienciaScripts

Imprint

Any brand names and product names mentioned in this book are subject to trademark, brand or patent protection and are trademarks or registered trademarks of their respective holders. The use of brand names, product names, common names, trade names, product descriptions etc. even without a particular marking in this work is in no way to be construed to mean that such names may be regarded as unrestricted in respect of trademark and brand protection legislation and could thus be used by anyone.

Cover image: www.ingimage.com

This book is a translation from the original published under ISBN 978-620-2-17995-9.

Publisher:
Sciencia Scripts
is a trademark of
Dodo Books Indian Ocean Ltd. and OmniScriptum S.R.L publishing group

120 High Road, East Finchley, London, N2 9ED, United Kingdom
Str. Armeneasca 28/1, office 1, Chisinau MD-2012, Republic of Moldova, Europe
Printed at: see last page
ISBN: 978-620-7-22311-4

Copyright © Dacyr Dante de Oliveira Gatto, Renato José Sassi
Copyright © 2024 Dodo Books Indian Ocean Ltd. and OmniScriptum S.R.L publishing group

I dedicate this study to my wife, my family and my work colleagues as a token of my gratitude for their support and coexistence.

ACKNOWLEDGEMENTS

I thank my wife for her concern and dedication.

To my family for their support during this research journey.

I would also like to thank my colleagues for their companionship and professionalism.

To the company I work for for their financial support.

Above all, I thank God for allowing me to fulfil my great desire to complete this stage of my life.

"Every victory conceals an abdication."

Simone de Beauvoir

SUMMARY

The aim of this research paper is to present a case study of a *software* development company, in which the *Software* Version Release Management process carried out for the client was analysed, as well as the problems that occurred in this execution during the period observed. In addition, the theoretical concepts of the processes contained in the ITIL library will be presented, with a focus on Release Management, and the concepts related to Business Process Management, according to the BPM methodology. This research also addresses how the theoretical contextualisation was applied to the company's processes, what tools were adopted, what results were obtained and whether the objective of structuring the processes and solving the problems encountered was achieved.

Keywords: Release Management, Business Process Management, ITIL, BPM.

CONTENTS

CHAPTER 1

INITIAL CONSIDERATIONS

1.1 Introduction

ITIL, the acronym for *Information Technology Infrastructure Library,* was initially developed by the *Central Computing and Telecommunications Agency* (CCTA), but is currently under the domain of the *Office of Government Commerce* (OGC). The OGC is a British government body that aims to develop methodologies and create standards within government departments, in order to improve internal processes. It consists of a coherent and integrated description of Information Technology (IT) Service Management practices. These practices help to implement and maintain management, focussing on people, processes and resources, which are used to deliver services that meet customer needs.

ITIL was created out of the need to standardise IT processes and based on the collective experience of various IT service management practitioners from private and public organisations around the world. This is the main reason why ITIL has become a reference standard in the area of service management, so that several leading organisations have already adopted this practice in their business segments on a global scale (MAGALHÃES & PINHEIRO, 2007).

1.2 Justification

As IT took on a strategic role within organisations, there was a need to know how processes could be mapped and managed efficiently and effectively. The advent of IT service management *frameworks*, such as ITIL, made it possible to gain a better understanding and guidance on what to do to solve problems encountered during process execution. With the implementation of ITIL, processes could be controlled and monitored, and targets and metrics imposed a quest for results within expectations.

1.3 Hypothesis

By applying the best practices proposed in ITIL, it is possible to control and monitor processes in order to eliminate faults and deliver value to the customer.

1.4 Research Objectives

1.4.1 General Objective

The aim of this work is to explore the processes contained in the ITIL library, with a focus on Release Management, using a case study of a *software* development company, whose problem in the software release process presented critical flaws that impacted on the business of both the client and the company, which generated rework and loss of quality in the final result.

1.4.2 Specific objectives

The specific objectives that served as the basis for this study were:

- To identify the deficiencies in the *software* development company's Version Release process, proposing improvements through the implementation of best practices and tools presented in the ITIL library;

- Follow the evolution of the company's Version Release process, from its unmanaged beginnings to the application of BPM tools for mapping process flows;

- With the processes known and mapped, apply the tools proposed in ITIL and obtain measurable and precise results, thus delivering value to the customer.

1.5 Characterising the problem

With the constant increase in the client's server fleet, to whom the *software* development company provides its services and products, the version release process, which used to be done manually, has become inaccurate and subject to distribution failures.

When distributing a unit or version release package for the system, the need arises to monitor, control and measure the distributions. It is therefore necessary to ensure that all servers receive the updates and are ready to be used by the workstations without any failures occurring in the distribution process.

CHAPTER 2

THEORETICAL FRAMEWORK

Nowadays, the aim of most organisations is to find solutions to improve IT services. The search for good practices and improvements in their processes has become essential in order to be competitive and achieve the desired success. As a result, methodologies have emerged to help organisations achieve better management of their IT services and infrastructure (SCHOENFELDER, 2010).

According to Schoenfelder (2010), IT cannot focus solely on technological issues, but must also be integrated with other areas of the organisation. In this way, IT Service Management has taken on a formal character and IT has become an investment within organisations and is no longer considered just a cost.

According to Magalhães and Pinheiros (2007), IT Service Management aims to guarantee the delivery of services that meet the requirements agreed between the supplier and the client, in terms of both performance and cost, as well as being aligned with the organisation's strategic objectives.

ITIL is a library of IT Service Management best practices that help to implement and maintain management, focusing on the people, processes and resources used to deliver these services. However, there is no specific description or steps to be followed on how these practices should be implemented, as each organisation has its own characteristics and particularities that should be known for greater adherence to ITIL. ITIL's approach lies in what to do, not how to do it. This characteristic makes it a *framework* and not a methodology (PINHEIRO, 2010).

The following is a contextualisation of the practices offered by the ITIL library, with a focus on Release Management in a real company, through a case study, showing how its use can lead to the solution of problems presented during the software version release process.

Concepts on the use of Business Process Management will be briefly addressed, since business and IT processes are closely linked and interact with each other in order to achieve corporate objectives (SILVA, 2006).

2.1 Business Process Management

A business process can be defined as an ordering of work activities in which space and time are used, together with a set of inputs and outputs. In other words, it is a set of activities that must be carried out in a certain order, in parallel or sequentially (DAVENPORT, 1994 apud SIQUEIRA, 2006).

Business Process Management, also known as *Business Process Management* (BMP), is a methodology for documenting, manipulating and formalising business processes, which broadens the view of the control flow and also has methods and tools to support projects (SANTOS et al., 2006).

2.1.1 Business Process Modelling

Business process modelling is a set of concepts, techniques and models aimed at developing and mapping an organisation's business model. The model produced is the result obtained by the company, after gathering relevant information, so that the business is fully understood (SANTOS et al., 2006).

Business modelling can map out existing processes, allowing problems to be identified and improvements to be made. In this way, it helps the organisation to understand its business clearly (SANTOS et al., 2006).

2.1.2 Benefits of BPM

According to Silva (2006), the benefits that organisations can gain from using BPM are:

- Improve business performance through understanding;

- Simulate new ways to serve the business;

- Supporting the organisation in relation to market fluctuations;

- Gain greater control over the duration of processes;

- Having a visual representation of the processes and their elements.

In the IT area, BPM also serves as a source of information for a wide range of activities such as identifying software requirements and defining integration solutions between companies (SILVA, 2006).

2.1.3 *Business Process Management Notation* (BPMN)

Developed by the *Business Process Management Initiative* (BPMI), the *Business Process Management Notation* (BPMN) was created to provide an easy notation that could be understood by all business users (SANTOS et al., 2006).

The elements that make up this process are divided into four categories: flow objects, connection objects, *swimlanes* and artefacts (SANTOS et al., 2006).

The flow objects are: events, activities and *gateways,* as can be seen in Figure 1.

Figure 1 - Flow Objects
Source: Correia, Leal & Almeida (2002)

The connection objects are: sequence flow, message flow and association (SANTOS et al., 2006):

These objects can be seen in Figure 2 below.

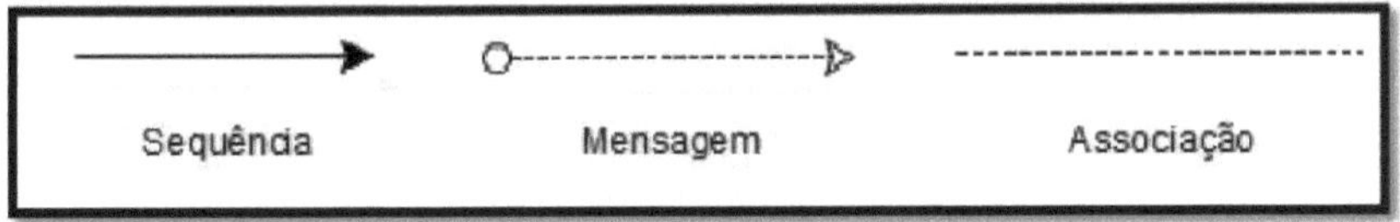

Figure 2 - Connection Objects
Source: Correia, Leal & Almeida (2002)

Swimlanes or lanes help with participation and the organisation of activities. As shown in Figure 3, *Pool* represents a participant in a process, while Lane is a subdivision within a lane used to organise and categorise activities (SANTOS et al., 2006).

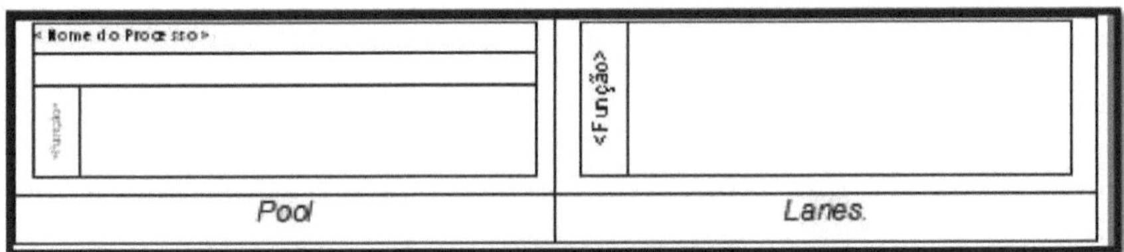

Figure 3 - *Swinlanes*
Source: Correia, Leal & Almeida (2002)

The artefacts are made up of *data* objects, which provide information about the activities that need to be carried out, annotation, which is a mechanism that provides additional information for the reader of the diagram, and the group, which is a set of activities that are within the same category (SANTOS et al., 2006).

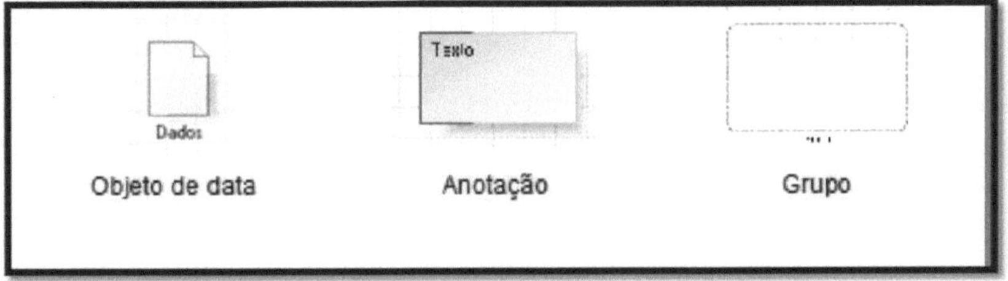

Figure 4 - Artefacts
Source: Correia, Leal & Almeida (2002)

2.2 Service Management

Most organisations use and depend on IT to be successful. If IT processes and services are properly implemented, managed and supported, the company will be successful, suffer fewer disruptions and lost productive

11

hours. In addition, it will reduce its costs, increase profits and improve public relations, thus more easily achieving its objectives (CARTLIDGE et al., 2007).

In short, Service Management is the management of the integration of people with processes and technology. It therefore aims to enable the delivery and support of services that are focused on customer needs, aligned with the business strategy, aiming for cost and performance between the IT area and other areas (MAGALHÃES & PINHEIRO, 2007).

According to Magalhães and Pinheiro (2007), Service Management is a specialised set of organisational skills for providing value to customers in the form of services.

In Service Management, the following terms are mentioned (MAGALHÃES & PINHEIRO, 2007):

- Service provider: an organisation that provides services to clients, whether internal or external;
- Customer: someone who buys goods or services;
- Business: an entity or organisation made up of a certain number of business units, in which the provider supplies services to a customer who is within the business;
- Service: is a means of delivering value to the customer, facilitating the results they want to achieve without having to assume costs and risks. To deliver value, the service has to work and fulfil what has been agreed with the customer;
- Functions: group of people and necessary and specialised resources that carry out one or more processes and activities;
- Roles: responsibilities defined in a process and assigned to a person or team, who can occupy more than one role;
- Process: a set of coordinated activities that produce a specific result and that, in some way, add value to the business;
- Responsibilities: commitment to your actions or to something entrusted

to you.

According to Magalhães and Pinheiro (2007), the characteristics that differentiate a service from a product are:

- Intangibility: a service cannot be tasted or touched;
- Indivisibility: cannot be separated from its provider;
- Variability: its quality can vary;
- Perishability: cannot be stored for later use.

2.2.1 Service Life Cycle

The Service Life Cycle is a model that presents a vision of its phases, from conception to the closure phase, in other words, it is how ITIL is structured (PINHEIRO, 2010).

According to Pinheiro (2010), the life cycle consists of five phases. These are:

- Service Strategy: conceptualises a set of services that help the business achieve its objectives. This is when strategic decisions are made about the services that will be developed;
- Service Design: designs the service, focusing on the objectives of usefulness and guarantee, based on what was decided in the strategy;
- Service Transition: moves services from the homologation environment to the production environment. Services are developed, tested and released in a controlled manner;
- Service Operation: manages services in production to ensure that their usefulness and guarantee objectives are met. Here, the day-to-day processes that keep the services running are considered;
- Continuous Service Improvement: evaluates services and identifies ways to improve them.

Continuous Service Improvement takes place simultaneously with all the other phases of the service life cycle (Pinheiro, 2010). Figure 5 illustrates this concept.

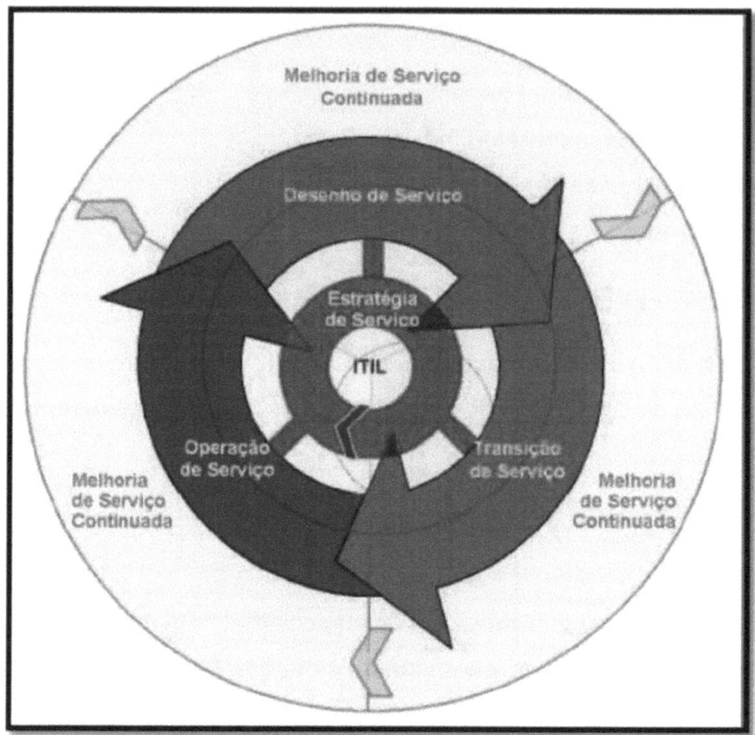

Figure 5 - Service Life Cycle
Source: Pinheiro (2010)

2.2.2 ITIL

The *Information Technology Infrastructure Library*, or simply ITIL, is a *framework* that brings together the most widely accepted IT management best practices in the world (GASPAR et al., 2010).

According to Gaspar et al. (2010), people currently adopt ITIL to obtain better results in terms of delivery and support for IT services, and it is the most widely used model for Service Management. Among the main reasons are:

- Non-proprietary model: can be used by any company, regardless of the technological platform;

- It's not a prescriptive model: it's a flexible model, meaning it can be adopted and adapted, and it doesn't depend on the size of the company or the sector;
- It provides good and best practices: companies benefit from this because they don't have to invest time in "reinventing the wheel";
- Used by thousands of companies around the world: it helps to establish a common terminology between internal and external IT providers;
- Helps meet the requirements of ISO/IEC 20000 (International Standard for IT Service Management).

The three main factors motivating the implementation of ITIL are the excellent results that good practices favour in terms of finances, quality and competitiveness (ANDRADE, 2008).

The implementation of these good practices brings positive results, mainly due to the fact that it is not linked to any technology or supplier (GASPAR et al., 2010).

According to Gaspar et al. (2010), the main focus of ITIL's good practices is to describe the processes needed to manage the entire IT infrastructure effectively and efficiently.

2.2.3 Concept of "Best Practice

Companies are looking to improve their processes in order to become more efficient and competitive. These innovations are successful if they are transformed into best practices. Over time, several companies begin to use them, turning them into good practices for companies in the sector. Over time, good practices become commonplace, ceasing to be a differentiator and becoming *commodities*. Practices considered necessary end up being incorporated into standards or regulatory requirements (GASPAR et al., 2010).

ITIL is based on IT governance best practices, which is formed by a reference model for implementing processes that use standardised terminology, thus defining a set of technical and operational activities (SILVA, 2006).

For Silva (2006), a "best practice" is the best result applied to real situations, i.e. a model that has been implemented after its relevance has been proven. This implementation is the ability to deploy models and experiences already acquired by other organisations, but adapted to the organisation.

The main objectives of ITIL's "best practices" are to improve performance and reduce costs. In addition, it provides indicators to strengthen IT environment management controls, which reduces execution time and service distribution (SILVA, 2006).

2.2.4 Benefits of Implementing ITIL

Below is a list of the most notable benefits when ITIL is implemented in an organisation (GASPAR et al., 2010):

- Practices that have already been approved, which saves time;

- More dynamic feedback on the implementation project;
- Improved quality of services for users and clients;
- Alignment of IT services with the needs of the organisation, both current and future;
- Increased customer satisfaction;
- Frequently motivated and focused team;
- More efficient and effective processes;
- Clearer vision and understanding of current capacity.

2.2.5 ITIL Concepts and Definitions

2.2.5.1 Service Strategy

Service Strategy is one of the phases of the process aimed at integrating IT into the business. This is when the IT department tries to understand the needs of its customers, whether internal or external. This phase also seeks to identify opportunities and risks, as well as deciding whether or not to outsource services and what return the organisation will get by making this investment (PINHEIRO, 2010).

According to Pinheiro (2010), as the IT department always has more service demands than it is able to fulfil, in this phase it is decided what the priorities will be for each of the tasks, as a demand will not always become a service. In this way, what is defined will be used in the design, development and implementation phases of service management.

The service strategy is made up of activities and processes in which the activities of market definition, development of strategic assets, offers and preparation for strategy execution stand out. The processes involved are (FILHO, 2011):

- Service portfolio management;
- Financial management;
- Demand management.

2.2.5.2 Service Design

In the Service Design phase, designs with quality, security and resilience must be produced for new or improved services. The strategic objectives defined in the previous phase are converted into portfolio services. The risks involved must be analysed, the necessary suppliers assessed and the capacity of the infrastructure to support the service understood (PINHEIRO, 2010).

At this point, it is necessary to consider everything that is needed to generate a service that meets the requirements and generates value for the customer, i.e. it is in the design that the quality objectives and targets are aligned so that the service is delivered within the necessary business conditions (PINHEIRO, 2010; GILI, 2009).

The design phase includes the following activities:

- Service catalogue management;
- Service level management;
- Capacity management;
- Availability management;
- IT service continuity management;
- Information security management;
- Supplier management.

2.2.5.3 Service Transition

This stage deals with planning and managing the transition of a service to the client's production environment. Here, the focus is on testing, measuring capacity and resources required, defining packages and deploying releases in the environment. At this stage, possible risks must be foreseen and plans drawn up for containment or setbacks should anything happen during the deployment of a service. It is also important to keep everyone involved informed, whether they are internal or external (GILI, 2009; PINHEIRO, 2010).

According to Gili (2009), one of the objectives that these controls are supposed to achieve is to increase customer satisfaction by minimising the impact that a change/implementation of a service can have on the customer's business. This phase links the service design and service operation phases.

The transition phase consists of the following activities (GILI, 2009):

- Change management;
- Configuration and service asset management;
- Release and deployment management;
- Service knowledge management;
- Transition planning and support;
- Service validation and testing.

2.2.5.4 Service Operation

Service Operation coordinates and carries out the activities and processes to deliver the service and manage it as agreed with the customer. This is the longest stage of the entire lifecycle, because here the service must be maintained until it is retired (taken out of the production environment). This phase represents day-to-day activities (FILHO, 2011).

At this stage, it is necessary to carry out some balances that are extremely important for maintaining a quality service and thus always guaranteeing customer satisfaction. According to Pinheiro (2010), these balances refer to:

- Internal and external vision of the business: it is not enough to have only the internal vision of what the service does and uses resources for, but to have the external vision (of the client) to know what is important and makes the service valuable to them;
- Stability and agility: if the team takes too long to stabilise a service when it becomes unavailable, it can damage the client's business and thus generate dissatisfaction. If, on the other hand, it's too fast, it can lead to a drop in quality and more failures due to a lack of planning;
- Quality and cost: customers demand high quality services all the time, but high quality can result in high costs. Therefore, you need to know how to use the resources you have to provide the best quality (be efficient);
- Reactive and proactive: a reactive team is always working to correct problems and this can give the customer a negative image. However, a team that is too proactive can increase operating costs to maintain the service.

The Service Operation phase represents the day-to-day life of the people involved with IT, while the other phases encompass the more tactical and strategic processes (FILHO, 2011). This stage is made up of the following processes:

- Event management;
- Incident management;
- Problem management;
- Access management;
- Execution of requisition.

2.2.5.5 Continuous Service Improvement

The Continuous Service Improvement phase of the life cycle implements improvements in each of the other phases, i.e. it seeks to improve the efficiency and effectiveness of processes and services (PINHEIRO, 2010).

The activities in this phase must be carried out in parallel with all the other phases, as each one generates outputs that are used as inputs for the next phase (FILHO, 2011).

This last phase is based on measurement, i.e. services and processes need to be implemented with well-defined objectives and targets, as well as their measurement. According to Pinheiro (2010), what should be understood about management and measurement is:

- You can't manage what you can't control;
- You can't control what you can't measure;
- You can't measure what you can't define.

2.2.5.6 PDCA model

ITIL recommends using the PDCA model for the Continuous Service Improvement process (FILHO, 2011).

Created by Willian Edwards Deming, PDCA is an interactive four-step management method used for the control and continuous improvement of processes (PINHEIRO, 2010).

According to Pinheiro (2010), the PDCA consists of four stages:

- *Plan*: identifies scope, objectives and requirements for the SBC;
- *Do*: allocates roles and responsibilities to work on MSC initiatives;
- *Check*: measures and reviews whether the SBC plan is being implemented and whether its objectives are being achieved;
- *Act*: is the decision to implement further improvements.

Figure 6 below shows the PDCA model in detail.

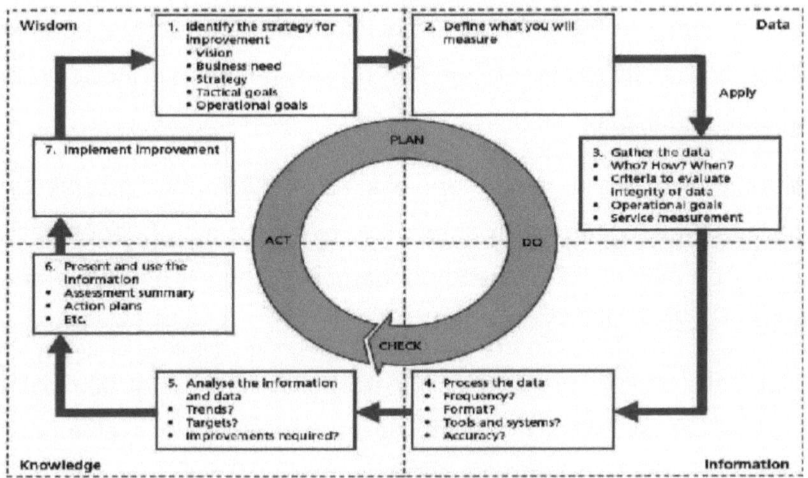

Figure 6 - PDCA model
Source: Cartlidge et al. (2007)

2.2.5.7 RACI matrix

The RACI matrix is a tool indicated by ITIL to help define an organisational structure. It also defines the roles and responsibilities of each individual in relation to the activities of a process (FILHO, 2011):

- *Responsible*: the role of the person carrying out the activity;
- *Accountable*: the role of the person who is ultimately responsible for the outcome of the decision or action related to the activity;
- *Consulted*: the role of the person who is involved before the decision or action is taken;

- *Informed*: the role of the person who needs to be informed after a decision or action, i.e. the person who needs to be kept up to date on the process of an activity.

2.2.6 Release Management

According to Pinheiro (2010), the Release Management process, which is part of the Service Transition stage, comes in at the final stage of the process, i.e. just after Change Management approves a change to release new versions of software into the production environment. Release Management will be concerned with all aspects related to the service release, including the training of users and support staff.

Release Management is the process responsible for implementing changes to the infrastructure environment, i.e. placing a set of configuration items that may be new or have already undergone changes and have been tested (MAGALHÃES & PINHEIRO, 2007).

This process defines the policies for releasing versions of all existing resources, as well as controlling the distribution of reliable versions, emergency changes and the frequency of updates (SILVA, 2006).

Release Management is responsible for introducing the changes that have been developed, tested and packaged into the production environment, and managing the other activities related to the release (MAGALHÃES & PINHEIRO, 2007).

The Release Management process is what "protects" the production environment, i.e. this is when formal procedures or exhaustive tests are carried out relating to changes in both software and hardware (HOLANDA, 2006).

According to Pinheiro (2010), the release process consists of the following activities:

- Planning: building a plan that should include scope, release content, risks, responsibilities and release stakeholders;

- Preparation for construction, testing and deployment: validation of the new or modified service based on the specifications;
- Construction and testing: management of the entire infrastructure and control of test environments;
- Service and pilot tests: checking components to see if they are working properly and are ready to be put into operation;
- Planning and preparation for deployment: checking the team is ready to start production;
- Transfer, implementation and withdrawal: business transition and operation;
- Verification of implementation: time to check that everything has gone according to plan;
- Support for the trial period: extra support that must be provided by the team responsible for the implementation.

2.2.6.1 The Four Stages of Release and Implementation

The objective of the Release and Implementation Management process is to plan, schedule and control the construction, testing and implementation of the release of new or modified services into the production environment, which will add value and fulfil business requirements (FILHO, 2011).

According to Pinheiro (2010), the four stages of release and implementation are:

- Release planning and implementation;
- Construction and testing of the release;
- Implementation;
- Review and closure.

2.2.6.2 Release Unit vs. Release Package

In Release Management, the terms Release Unit and Release Package are often used. A Release Unit is a small quantity of a service that is released according to the release policy adopted. These small quantities can vary according to the service, i.e. the whole system can be released or just a module (PINHEIRO, 2010).

A Release Package is a set of release units or even a single unit. A new version of software may be released containing the new application, database *script* and user manuals, for example. This set is a release package (PINHEIRO, 2010).

2.2.6.3 Paper

According to Pinheiro (2010), there are roles, i.e. those responsible for release management in each of its phases. The first role is that of the "release manager" who is responsible for planning, designing, building, configuring and testing the release package.

The "release packaging and construction manager" is responsible for establishing the final configuration of the release. Finally, the "implementation team" is responsible for the delivery/physical implementation of the service/component (PINHEIRO, 2010).

2.2.6.4 Key Performance Indicators (KPIs)

Key Performance Indicators (KPI) are stipulated to measure the level of performance of a process. Consequently, these indicators determine whether different actions need to be taken to improve the current results. Key Performance Indicators should only be changed if a company's primary objectives also change (PINHEIRO, 2010).

In release management, we can have KPIs (FILHO, 2011):

- Number of changes successfully implemented;
- Reduction in the number of unauthorised changes;
- Reduction in the number of accumulated change requests;
- Reduction in the number and percentage of unplanned changes and emergency corrections;
- Reduction in the number of failed changes.

2.2.6.5 Configuration Management System (CMS)

A configuration item is any component that needs to be managed to ensure the delivery of an IT service (PINHEIRO, 2010).

Also according to Pinheiro (2010), the Configuration Management System (CMS) is responsible for maintaining information on configuration items required in the delivery of an IT service, including their relationships.

CHAPTER 3

RESEARCH METHODOLOGY

For the preparation of this work, literature (works, academic papers and *websites*) on the subject of ITIL and BPM was used, since theoretical knowledge on the subject is essential in order to contextualise, analyse and direct the events observed in the case study of this research.

This study includes, among its technical procedures, the bibliographical research mentioned above, documentary research, which is a survey of data based on focussed interviews, and above all the case study of the *software* development company.

For the documentary research, documents, spreadsheets and tools used by the team responsible for administering the procedures studied were used, linking them to the theory researched in the bibliography.Regarding the case study, the qualitative research methodology was used, collecting data, observing the environment, participating and interacting with the members of the situations investigated, taking notes on the behaviour observed, as well as its results, by monitoring the activities between April 2013 and April 2014.Surveys were also carried out with members of the team investigated, in the form of focused interviews, collecting technical and procedural information that impacted or influenced the processes analysed in the case study.

CHAPTER 4

CASE STUDY

4.1 Company presentation

The *software* development company that is the focus of this study is a software factory located in the south of the country that supplies its solutions to clients in all Brazilian states, Latin America and the United States (SOFTPLAN, 2014).

Operating since 1990 in various market segments, such as justice, infrastructure and works, public management, projects co-financed by international organisations and the construction industry, the *software* developer has a contingent of more than 1,500 employees who work in its regional headquarters and are allocated to its clients (SOFTPLAN, 2014).

The focus will be on *software in* the Justice area, delivered to its client in São Paulo, where the number of users exceeds 70,000. This study will show the problem that the application infrastructure team, allocated to the client, encountered in carrying out the *software* release process, the search for ITIL-focused solutions, the application of its tools, and the solution found so that the company's objectives with the client were achieved.

4.2 The Initial Scenario

The product delivered to the client consists of a client-server software solution distributed on a fleet of servers classified as mentioned below:

- Application servers: large servers located in *datacentres,* responsible for connecting the applications on the workstations to the database servers;
- Edge servers: small servers, located at the customer's physical location, which serve as a repository for distributing release packages;
- Database servers: servers on which database instances are configured

and executed.

The application works by having its objects (executables, libraries, help files and other objects) distributed between the application servers and the edge servers.

The concept of edge servers works like a central server at the physical location of the workstations so that when there is a version update, the workstations receive the update quickly directly from the edge server, without burdening the infrastructure at the location, for example by overloading the data *link* when transmitting objects to all the workstations.

4.3 The Problem Found

In quantitative terms, the client has 197 application servers and 502 edge servers which, during the version release process, must be fed with the version objects and be ready for use as soon as the procedure is finalised. There are also 21 database servers, where the parameter and table configuration *scripts* are executed so that the databases are adapted to each software version. Figure 7 illustrates the basic communication scheme between the servers.

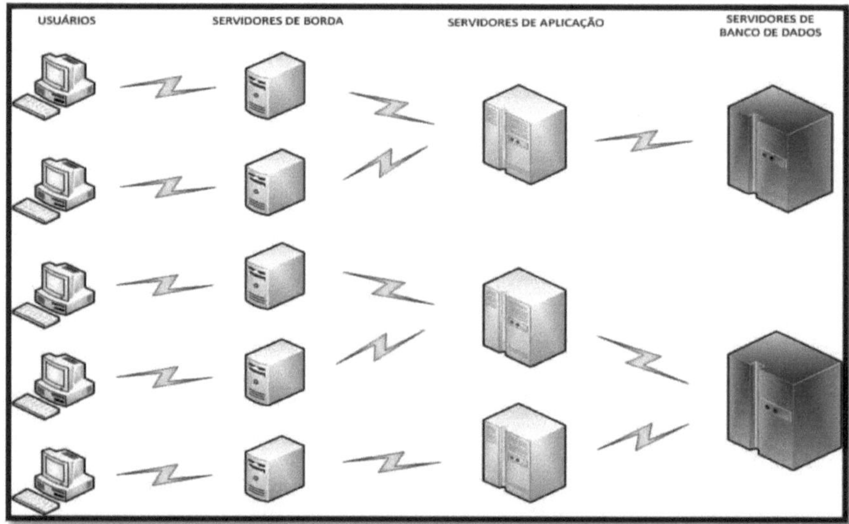

Figure 7 - Basic Communication Topology between Application, Edge and Database Servers

In order to understand what the release process was like before ITIL best practices were implemented, in this particular process, here is a description of how the activities were carried out:

When a software version was released from the homologation phase, it was sent to the application infrastructure team to carry out the update activity after office hours.

For the version to be successfully distributed and released, the activity depended on the following steps being carried out:

- Stop the application services on the application servers;
- Delete a defined folder structure within each application server, as the files from the old version would no longer be useful and, if they remained on the servers, could cause a conflict with the new version;
- Transferring the objects directed at the application servers, which consisted of executables, libraries, information documents, etc;
- Transfer the objects directed at the edge servers, as well as the application servers, each with its own particularities;
- Configure system parameters;
- Execute the database *scripts;*
- Upload the application services to the application servers;
- Test the connectivity of each application.

The fulfilment of these steps is essential for the perfect functioning of the system.

Previously, when the server fleet consisted of only a few machines, the updating work could be done manually, machine by machine, and this met expectations. However, as already mentioned, the server park became large, and the distribution of these objects and the execution of *scripts did* not follow any documented criteria or defined process. What's more, it was carried out by employees who, despite having technical knowledge, got lost in the management of the activity due to the continuous increase in its proportion.

Whenever work started on the client, the result was catastrophic, as the application servers did not have the correct versions, the edge servers were not up to date, which made it impossible to update several workstations, and the *scripts were executed with* errors or not at all, preventing several users from carrying out their activities, as the application did not work properly and often did not even start.

As a result, the team monitoring the start of the day had to identify and update each server manually and on time, as well as analysing whether any *scripts* had failed to run, which took almost a whole day or more, causing a negative impact on the client and also on the team's other daily activities.

Faced with this scenario, what happened during the release of the version to all the interested areas, as this situation was repeated, causing enormous inconvenience? The following situations were observed:

- Only one analyst on the team was responsible for all the object transfers to all the servers, whether they were application servers or edge servers;
- The transfers were carried out using a batch file for each type of server with the IP addresses of each machine. As soon as the file was executed, the server-to-server transfer began, but there was no confirmation as to whether the transfer had been successfully carried out;
- New servers were always added to the park by the client, but there was no control over them, which led to several cases of outdated servers in each activity, because they weren't mapped in time in the batch file;
- Several edge servers were switched off by the client at the end of each location's working day, which meant that they could no longer be updated during the activity;
- *Scripts weren*'t executed correctly or simply weren't executed at all, and

some database servers lacked parameterisation.

Given the above, the following question remains: would it be possible to implement a methodology or apply an IT management *framework in* order to gain control of the Software Version Release process at the company in question and correct the flaws that were damaging the client's and the organisation's business, as well as its image?

4.4 Implementing Best Practices

The company's image vis-à-vis the client had been eroded, which led to numerous breaches of contract and the failure of the *software* developer to meet deadlines.

As a result, the company and the team responsible for this process needed to be urgently restructured, since the already dissatisfied client would be terminating the contract permanently if no solution was found to the problem.

The company then set about restructuring its employees, processes and technologies, seeking guidance from the ITIL library and process modelling methodologies such as BPM.

An ITIL-certified coordinator was then appointed. He chose employees who were also certified so that they could research which best practices in this *framework* would suit the reality that the infrastructure area was experiencing at the time.

By analysing the scenario, it was possible to see the need to implement practices that would coordinate the stages of the process from strategy, design, transition and operation, in order to achieve a manageable and measurable result.

Using the ITIL library, especially the book "Service Transition, Focusing on the Release and Deployment Management Process", we sought guidance on how to organise the process. ITIL, being a structural *framework*, allows other techniques and processes from *frameworks to* be used together. This allowed techniques from the BPM methodology to be used for mapping the process and subsequently its sub-processes.

The best practices adopted are presented below.

A catalogue of services was drawn up to make it clear what the team's activities were and where attention should be focused in order to improve the techniques and processes that should receive the most attention. In this catalogue, it was made clear which activities would be the team's responsibilities, including version release management;

Control of configuration items was also created, so that all servers (application, edge and database) were mapped, and the information was updated daily. In a simple way, the information on all the servers (IPs, *hostnames*, *ranges*, physical addresses of the locations, etc.) was centralised in a spreadsheet in the cloud (where all interested parties could have constant access to the information). This resource plays the role of a configuration management system, as illustrated in Figure 8.

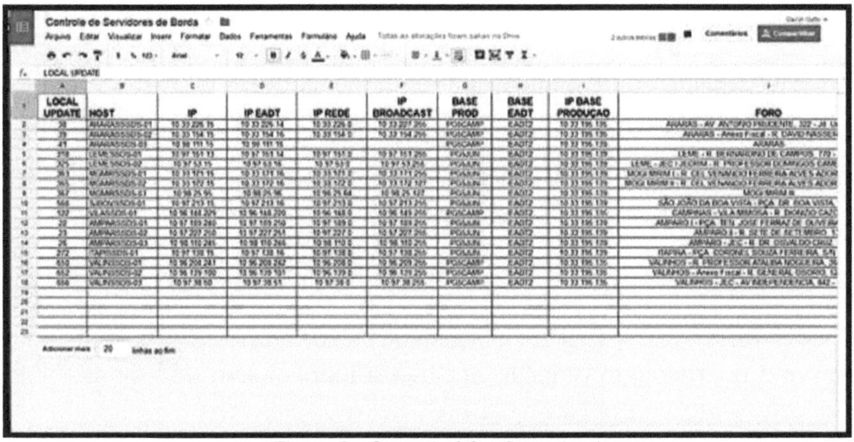

Figure 8 - Control of Configuration Items

Source: Softplan (2014)

The roles or people responsible for this process were also defined: a person responsible for releasing and implementing each type of server (edge and application); a person responsible for running *scripts* on the database servers; a person responsible for drawing up a catalogue of configuration items, where each application, edge and database server that was part of the server park would be documented and registered, each according to their knowledge and expertise on the subject and the *framework*.

Process flows were defined, using the BPM methodology shown in this paper, making it clear what the responsibilities of each team member were, as well as the flow to be followed, so that each stage of the process was clear.

A matrix of responsibilities (RACI Matrix) was drawn up. The RACI Matrix made it possible to define those responsible, accountable, consulted and informed throughout the process. Table 1 illustrates this tool.

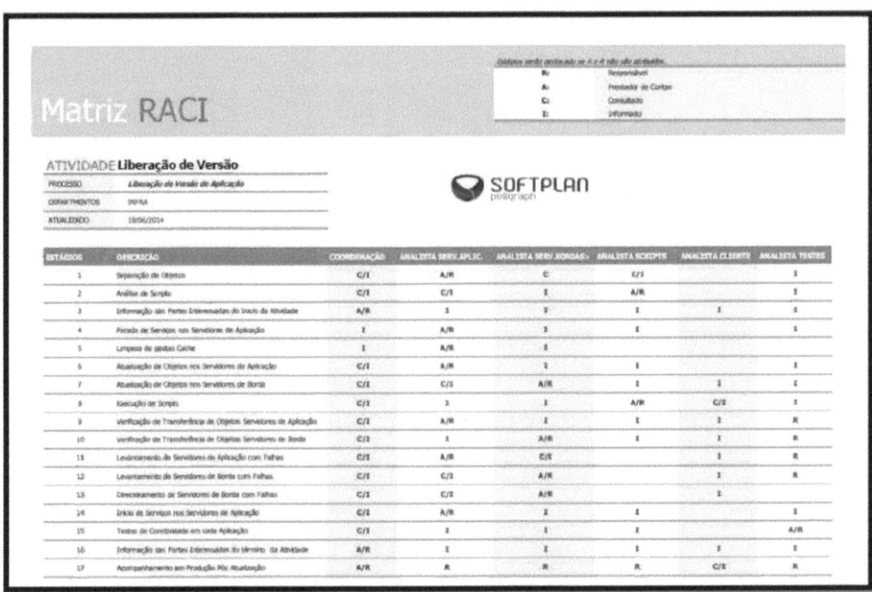

Matriz RACI

ATIVIDADE **Liberação de Versão**

PROCESSO: Liberação de Versão de Aplicação
DEPARTAMENTOS: INFRA
ATUALIZADO: 18/06/2014

SOFTPLAN

R:	Responsável
A:	Prestador de Contas
C:	Consultado
I:	Informado

ESTÁGIOS	DESCRIÇÃO	COORDENAÇÃO	ANALISTA SERV.APLIC.	ANALISTA SERV.BORDAS>	ANALISTA SCRIPTS	ANALISTA CLIENTE	ANALISTA TESTES
1	Separação de Objetos	C/I	A/R	C	C/I		I
2	Análise de Scripts	C/I	C/I	I	A/R		I
3	Informação das Partes Interessadas do Início da Atividade	A/R	I	I	I	I	I
4	Parada de Serviços nos Servidores de Aplicação	I	A/R	I	I		I
5	Limpeza de pastas Cache	I	A/R	I			
6	Atualização de Objetos nos Servidores de Aplicação	C/I	A/R	I	I		I
7	Atualização de Objetos nos Servidores de Borda	C/I	C/I	A/R	I	I	I
8	Execução de Scripts	C/I	I	I	A/R	C/I	I
9	Verificação de Transferência de Objetos Servidores de Aplicação	C/I	A/R	I	I	I	R
10	Verificação de Transferência de Objetos Servidores de Borda	C/I	I	A/R	I	I	R
11	Levantamento de Servidores de Aplicação com Falhas	C/I	A/R	C/I		I	R
12	Levantamento de Servidores de Borda com Falhas	C/I	C/I	A/R		I	R
13	Direcionamento de Servidores de Borda com Falhas	C/I	C/I	A/R		I	
14	Início de Serviços nos Servidores de Aplicação	C/I	A/R	I	I		I
15	Testes de Conectividade em cada Aplicação	C/I	I	I	I		A/R
16	Informação das Partes Interessadas do Término da Atividade	A/R	I	I	I	I	I
17	Acompanhamento em Produção Pós Atualização	A/R	R	R	R	C/I	R

Table 1 - RACI Matrix Used in the Version Release Process
Source: Softplan (2014)

Using the four ITIL release stages, the process was planned, programmed and controlled. It was therefore decided that the strategies for the release activities would be carried out in a coordinated and continuous manner between the new people responsible for the tasks and, once they had been completed, they would be reviewed in order to eliminate execution errors. The flows created with the help of the BPM methodology provided the necessary visualisation for the strategies to be created, as can be seen in Figure 9:

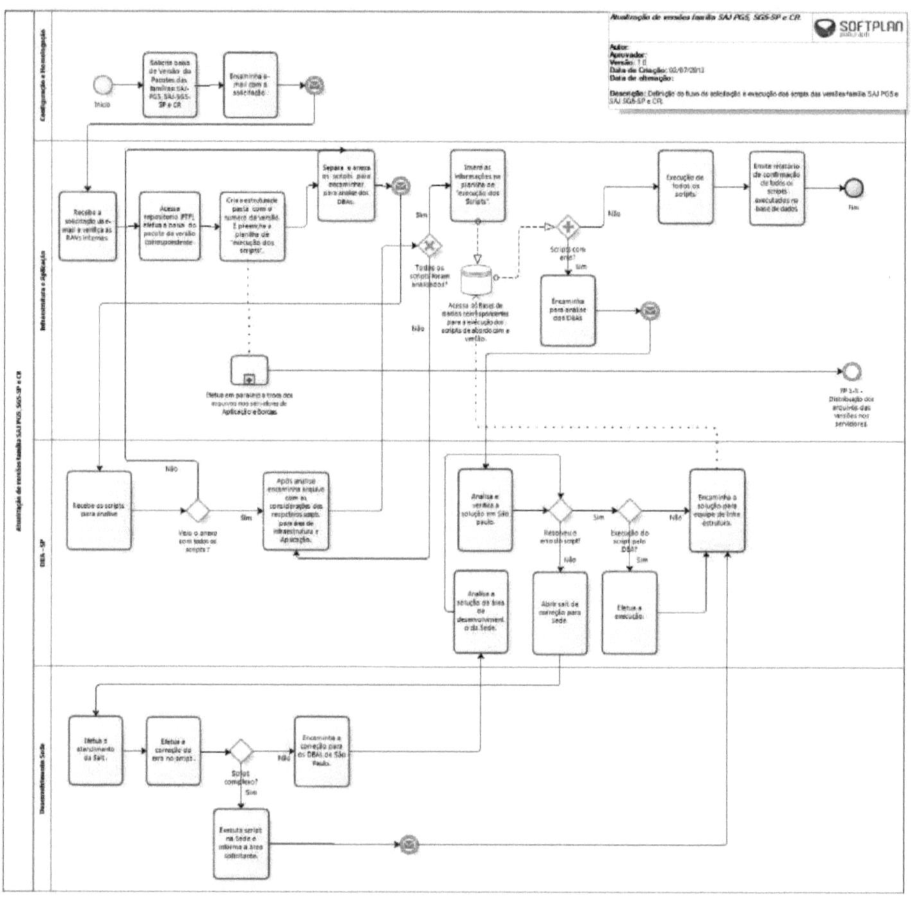

Figure 9 - Version Release Process Flow
Source: Softplan (2014)

Based on the PDCA mentioned in ITIL, a tool was implemented that would automatically distribute the edge servers, generating assertiveness *logs* and indicating which servers had failed. This would generate a contingency plan for updating them before they were released into production.

The software, known internally as *Console,* was developed by the company's development team to replace the initial batch files and the edge servers to distribute the objects simultaneously to all locations. Figure 10 shows the application's main screen.

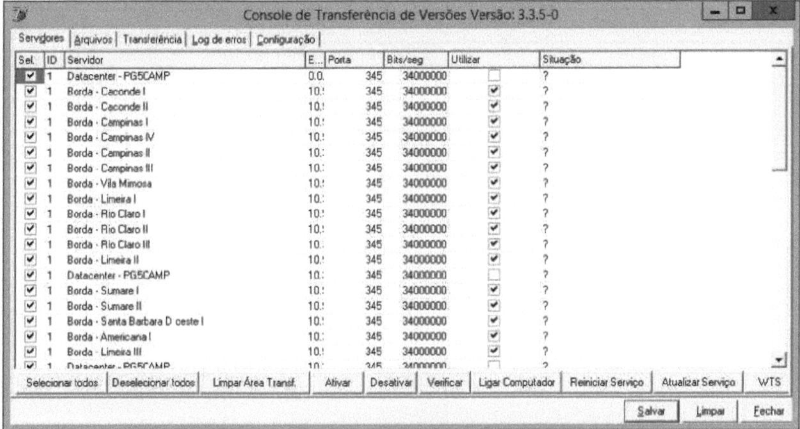

Figure 10 - Version Transfer *Console* Application Screen

Source: Softplan (2014)

4.5 Obtaining and Measuring Results

According to the ITIL definition, every process is measurable, so it was necessary to draw up metrics to assess whether or not the release process achieved its objective. Key performance indicators (KPIs) were also stipulated to judge the efficiency and effectiveness of the process.

The initial metrics were to identify, at the time of the version update, how many and which servers (application and edge) were unavailable. The complexity of the version to be released was then measured by the number of objects to be transferred, as well as the number of *scripts to* be executed. Tables 2 and 3 show examples of the metrics used to measure the processes.

| Atualização PG | | | | | | | |
Versão	Objetos	Servidores de Aplicação	Servidores de Borda	Servidores Aplicação com Falhas Durante Atualização	Servidores de Borda com Falhas Durante Atualização	Servidores Aplicação com Falhas Pós Atualização	Servidores de Borda com Falhas Pós Atualização
1.5.21-24-A	28	197	500	0	15	0	0
1.5.21-24-B	4	179	0	3	0	0	0
1.5.21-24-D	4	179	0	2	0	0	0
1.5.21-26	17	197	500	0	8	0	0
1.5.21-26A	6	179	500	17	4	0	0
1.5.21-27	18	197	500	0	7	0	0
1.5.21-29	17	197	500	1	11	0	0
1.5.23-6	36	197	500	0	4	0	0
1.5.23-7	18	197	500	1	4	0	0
1.5.23-7_B	7	197	0	0	0	0	0
Atualização SG							
Versão	Objetos	Servidores de Aplicação	Servidores de Borda	Servidores Aplicação com Falhas Durante Atualização	Servidores de Borda com Falhas Durante Atualização	Servidores Aplicação com Falhas Pós Atualização	Servidores de Borda com Falhas Pós Atualização
1.7.12-6	26	37	18	0	0	0	0
1.7.12-8	12	37	18	0	0	0	0

Table 2 - Edge and Application Server Fault Control

Source: Softplan (2014)

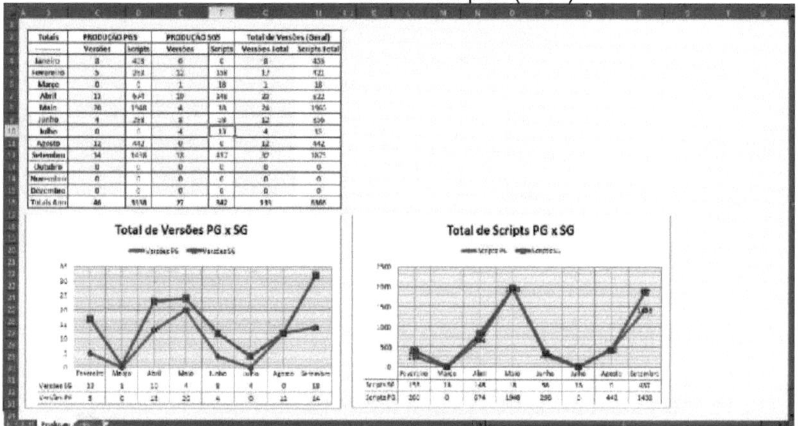

Table 3 - Object and *Script* Control

Source: Softplan (2014)

With the results in hand, it was possible to create sub-processes, with the aim of directing the updating of workstations to workstation servers.

The main servers were recovered and released for updating.

Now, with the control of configuration items in place, it was possible to be aware of all the active and operational servers. If any were activated or deactivated, there was daily control to manage the servers.

The whole process has been perfected, so that even the time taken to carry out the version update steps has been reduced.

In less than six months, control of the process was obtained, so that it could be managed and measured. These results were presented to the client, taking into account both the quality and value of the service, since the users' work was no longer affected by the version release process, which became transparent to them.

4.6 Next steps

The company is aware of the need to keep current processes evolving, always seeking to improve them, especially in relation to the control tools created with the aim of drawing up and maintaining a historical project base, which will help with future projects.

It has become a constant concern of the company to maintain processes and monitor their application, in order to guarantee the quality of the activities carried out. For this reason, the company is always looking for qualifications for its employees, which proved to be fundamental in the study presented.

CHAPTER 5

CONCLUSIONS

5.1 Final considerations

The study presented showed the implementation of ITIL best practices in the Application Infrastructure sector of a *software* development company, with the aim of organising its processes and improving performance in IT management.

As the problems with the quality of the services provided by the company were related to a series of change activities carried out in a disorganised way, without planning and without measurement, it was noted that there was a need to establish flows for the processes and to manage and measure, through controls, whether the objectives would be achieved with quality and in an efficient manner.

It was also noted that the initial knowledge of the employees involved was fundamental to the correct interpretation and application of the best practices presented throughout the ITIL library, especially the Release and Implementation Management process. The distribution of responsibilities in a coordinated manner meant that activities and their tasks could be carried out in an organised manner, being reviewed and corrected in good time before releasing to production.

Currently, the process has its steps documented and is easy to understand for all parties interested in the Software Release Management that the company carries out, including the client who, in addition to following the process from start to delivery, has been satisfied with the results obtained, since the number of failures in the transfer of release packages has reached 0.

Finally, it can be concluded that the best practices proposed in ITIL have made it possible to map, control and monitor processes efficiently and effectively, achieving a level of quality never before achieved.

5.2 Recommendations for future work

Continually reviewing IT processes, as recommended by the PDCA, can lead the company to develop new working methods in order to increase productivity in IT service management, with the aim of continually increasing quality and reducing the cost of processes, which guarantees the organisation a return on its investment.

CHAPTER 6

REFERENCES

ANDRADE, J. N. **A Process for Implementing ITIL Practices for IT Service Management.** Master's dissertation in Computer Science, Federal University of Pernambuco, Recife/PE, 2008. Available at: <http://www.4hd.com.br/files/200907-tcc-jeime.zip>. Accessed on: 21 September 2014.

CARTLIDGE, A.; HANNA; A. RUDD, C.; MACFARLANE, I.; WINDEBANK, J.; RANCE, S. **An Introductory Overview of ITIL® V3.** 2007. Available at: <http://www.best-managementpractice.com/gempdf/itSMF_An_Introductory_Overview_of_ITIL _V3.pdf>. Accessed on: 20 September 2014.

CORREIA, K. S. A.; LEAL, F.; ALMEIDA, D. A. Process Mapping: an approach for analysing business processes. **XXII National Production Engineering Meeting**. Curitiba. 2002.

FILHO, F. C. **ITIL - Information Technology Infrastructure Library**. Rio de Janeiro: Escola Superior de Redes, 2011. Available at: <http://pt.scribd.com/doc/50809607/47/Operacao-de-Servico>. Accessed on: 19 September 2014.

GASPAR, M.; GOMEZ, T.; MIRANDA, Z. **T.I. Change and Innovation: Resolving conflicts with ITIL V3 - applied to a case study**. Brasília: Senac, 2010.

GILI, D. P. **A study of PMBOK® and ITIL®.** Monograph (Graduation) in Computer Science from the State University of Londrina, Londrina/PR, 2009. Available at:

<http://www.gaia.uel.br/media/uploads/gaia/TCC_Diogo.pdf>. Accessed on: 21 September 2014.

HOLANDA, I. D. **Fundamentals of IT service management:** based on ITIL. Holland. 2006.

MAGALHÃES, I. L.; PINHEIRO, W. B. **IT Service Management in Practice:** an approach based on ITIL®. 1ª ed. Novatec, 2007.

PINHEIRO, F. R. **Fundamentals of IT Service Management based on ITIL® V3**. 2010.

SANTOS, A. G.; CRUZ, G. M.; SANTANA, M. R. **Business Process Modelling for Government Agencies**. Monograph for the Software Residency Programme, Salvador/BA, 2006. Available at: <svn2.assembla.com/svn/projeto_pri/MonografiaResidentesDCC.pdf>. Accessed on: 20 September 2014.

SCHOENFELDER, K. **Change Management System based on ITIL Best Practices**. Monograph (Graduation) in Information Systems by the Regional University of Blumenau, Blumenau/SC, 2010. Available at: <http://campeche.inf.furb.br/tccs/2010-I/TCC2010-1-15-VF-KarinSchoenfelder.pdf> Accessed on: 14 Sep. 2014.

SILVA, J. B. **Integration between BPM and ITIL - Case study at the Federal University of Bahia**. Monograph for the Software Residency Programme, Salvador/BA, 2006. Available at: <http://www.wepapers.com/Papers/45551/Integra%C3%A7%C3%A3o_entr

e_BPM_e_ITIL_-
_Case_Study_at_the_Federal_University_of_Bahia>. Accessed on: 15 September 2014.

SIQUEIRA, A. V. **Business Process Modelling**. Monograph (Graduation) by the Institute of Mathematics and Statistics of the University of São Paulo, São Paulo, 2006. Available at:

<http://www.vision.ime.usp.br/~andy/mac499/avsiqueira_monografia.pdf>. Accessed on: 15 September 2014.

SOFTPLAN. Santa Catarina, 2014. Available at: <http://www.softplan.com.br/a-softplan/quem-somos/> Accessed on: 20 September 2014.

I want morebooks!

Buy your books fast and straightforward online - at one of world's fastest growing online book stores! Environmentally sound due to Print-on-Demand technologies.

Buy your books online at
www.morebooks.shop

Kaufen Sie Ihre Bücher schnell und unkompliziert online – auf einer der am schnellsten wachsenden Buchhandelsplattformen weltweit! Dank Print-On-Demand umwelt- und ressourcenschonend produzi ert.

Bücher schneller online kaufen
www.morebooks.shop